HEALING - THE SHAMAN'S WAY
BOOK 3- Using Herbs

I0085224

Norman W. Wilson PhD

HEALING - THE SHAMAN'S WAY
BOOK 3 – Using Herbs

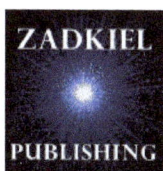

ZADKIEL

PUBLISHING

Cover Design by

www.srwalkerdesigns.com

Interior Photography by
Suzanne V. Wilson Photography

DISCLAIMER

There are no guarantees that any of the procedures or suggestions described herein will work. Before following the use of any of these suggestions always consult your medical practitioner. Persons under the age of eighteen should not attempt any of these activities. Please remember you are responsible for how you use the information contained in this book.

Norman W. Wilson, PhD

10/22/2022

APPRECIATION

I am deeply appreciative of the faith, help, and encouragement I have received from each of the following: Stuart Holland, my editor and publisher, Stephen R. Walker for cover design, Omar Lopez for interior graphics and videos, and especially my wife, Suzanne V Wilson for the use of her photos and continued support.

CHAPTER ONE
OVERVIEW

Please note that the following material is suggestive and is not intended to replace modern medical practices. Always check with your doctor before using any of the herbs discussed in this course. Even though the Food and Drug Administration requires manufacturers of dietary supplements to ensure their products are free of contaminants is not a guarantee of their safety. And that includes herbs.

Some of you may be taking this stand-alone course without having taken the first course, 'Healing-The Shaman's Way." I will reshare some of the information from that course, especially from Lecture 4, "Healing From Mother Earth-Part One-Herbs"

The first verifiable evidence of the medicinal use of herbs dates back to 70,000 years ago, with the discovery of ten mummified bodies in the Shanidar Cave, Iraq.

The fourth mummified body had the following plants: Yarrow, Cornflower, Batchelor's Button, St. Barnaby's Thistle, Ragwort, Marshmallow, Grape Hyacinth, and Hollyhock. That discovery was in 1960.

However, the first concrete evidence for the use of plants for healing purposes came to light in 1991 with the discovery of a 5,300-years-old frozen man. Otzi, as he has been named, carried what is called a medicine bag which contained two chunks of the mushroom, Piptoporus betulinus, or birch bracket as it is commonly called. This particular mushroom is used to fight an intestinal parasite.

An autopsy showed Otzi had an intestinal parasite.

Shamans of old and today believe that all things are connected and there is a corresponding relationship to the world of healing. Fundamental to this belief is the use of medicinal plants. Plant Medicine quickly became the treatment du jour. The shaman's role is to diagnose, recommend treatment, and provide treatment. Over 2,000 pants have been identified as useable medicinal plants. Remember, all plants are not herbs. What then is an herb?

Herbs are the green leafy part of a plant and can be used to support the respiratory system, as an expectorant, soothes nasal passages, fights harmful organisms, and help the healing processes in a variety of human physical and emotional issues. The leaves of plants, trees, and shrubs can be used to aid in the healing process. And that includes herbs.

The usable parts of herbs can be flower buds, leaves, stems, roots, or bark, woody parts of a whole plant. All of these may be prepared as the following:

- A decoction is used for herbs and plants that are not easily chewable; Pine needles for example. Grind these using a mortar and pestle or a coffee grinder
- Powder is made by grinding dried herbs and plants
- Syrups are made from ground herbs and plants. They are then dissolved in water. Sometimes the syrup is bitter. To offset the bitterness had a teaspoon of raw honey.
- Salves/Ointments/balms are made with ground herbs/plants and added to a base such as a beeswax
- Sprays are made with the herb leaves boiled in water
- Teas are made with herbs either ground or chopped and boiling water
- Soups are made with a variety of vegetables, meats, seafood, and herbs

For those who prefer to make herbal medicines here is a partial list of things you will need the following items:

- Saucepans (at least a couple of different sizes), sterilized
- Stainless steel spoons (long-handled, slotted, and non-slotted)
- Stainless steel spatulas

- Sterilized jars, lids, and plastic containers of various sizes
- Mortar/pestle, or an electric grinder)
- Knives (one for paring, cutting, and chopping)
- Strainers and cheesecloth

As with crystals, some herbs are potentially harmful and should be avoided or used with care. Here is a partial list:

•	Comfrey, Sassafras,	Pennyroyal, Ephedra
•	Betel Nut, Mistletoe,	Red Sage, Gingko
•	Farfarae, Hawthorn,	Bear Berry, Bitter Orange
•	Conker, Lobelia,	Kava, St John's Wort

To eliminate any confusion about herbs and herbals an herb is a physical plant and or its parts; whereas, an herbal may be parts of the plant with other substances added. Spices are the roots of the plant. Only herbs will be discussed in this course.

Here are some general considerations when using herbs:

1. Many herbs are used in teas. Avoid adding more than suggested in the recipe and don't over steep

2. Pregnant women, breastfeeding mothers, infants, and very young children should not use herbs

3. Even though an herb recipe did not work for you, using it could delay getting medical treatment

4. Some herbs can produce unexpected and negative side effects.

5. Hemp and marijuana are of the same plant species. Hemp's legal definition is that it is a cannabis plant containing 0.3 percent or less of THC On the other hand, marijuana, is also a cannabis plant containing more than 0.3 percent THC. Hemp is considered an herb.

Botanical medicine, phytomedicine, and herbalism all refer to herb-based medicine. Further, many of today's drugs are now plant-based. Opium, quinine, digitalis, and aspirin. Aspirin for example is made from Willow Bark.

Please remember, that it is not recommended that you ignore modern medical practices. Burke Lennihan reminds us that "Medicinal herbs contain many beneficial chemical compounds that provide a versatile array of therapeutic powers." (BurkeLennihan. *The Practical Herbal Medicine Handbook*. NY. Fall River Press, 2014 P 441). An example of a plant rich in flavonoids is Hawthorn. Among other things, Hawthorn is known to help blood flow.

It's estimated that somewhere between 50 thousand to 80 thousand plant species have medicinal value. A small fraction of that number has been explored and developed.

CHAPTER TWO
USING HERBS FOR TEAS

Herb teas are called herbal infusions. A less-known term is tisanes. The earliest record of herb tea is from 2737 BCE in China. Herb Teas spread from China to Egypt and Japan. The Dutch were mainly responsible for trading tea with other European countries and beyond. William H. Ukers in his 1934 book titled *About Tea* reminds us that the word "tea" is not found in the Bible. Furthermore, he states it is not found in any of the works by Shakespeare. It is not found in any book or publication previous to the 1650s.

What then, is tea? *Tea* is an aromatic beverage usually prepared by pouring boiling water over cured or fresh plant leaves. Some authorities list three major types of teas while others list as many as nine. Herb tea is listed as a type; however, traditionalists hold to the idea that tea is a beverage made exclusively from Camellia Sinensis. The following teas are created from the Camellia Sinensis plant:

- Black Tea   Green Tea   Oolong Tea
- Pu-erh   Yellow Tea   White Tea

Teas' general benefits for human beings include the following:

- Protects against cardiovascular issues
- Helps regulate Type 2 diabetes
- Helps lower blood pressure
- Helps lower cholesterol
- Protects the body against free radicals generated by pollution
- Targets and prevents cancer cells from developing

With over 3,000 varieties of tea, it becomes an impossible task to deal with all of them in this course. One list, for example, provides 29 different kinds of green tea. Modern teas are made from leaves, roots, seeds, needles, and bark of a wide variety of plants. Even though Herb is listed as a type of tea, it is not viewed as a real tea but as an infusion. Much of a tea's value as nutrition for your immune system depends on the soil in which the herbs are grown.

What is an herb and is it different from spice? An herb is a plant that has aromatic qualities. Most may be used as seasonings in food as well as for medicinal purposes. The basic difference between an herb and a spice rests with what parts of the plant are taken- the leaf or other green part of a plant. All other parts of a plant including the roots, berries, seeds, twigs, needles, and bark are considered spices. Cinnamon comes from the bark of a tree; it, therefore, is classified as a spice. On the other hand, Parsley comes from the plant's leaves and is an herb. However, for our purposes here, we will call all of them herbs. Herbs can be and are often used to help cure or provide relief to many of our physical, mental, and emotional issues.

Seven common herbs have been selected as examples. Recipes for the teas are in a booklet titled A Booklet of Teas available in Resources. It is free and can be downloaded.

Chamomile

Chamomile is one of the oldest herbs known to humankind. Among medicinal plants is often called the "Star". There are two common varieties: German Chamomile and Roman Chamomile. There are many different preparations for Chamomile but the most popular form is that of tea with more than a million cups consumed per day.

Chamomile has been used to treat many physical and emotional conditions. Among these are the following:

- Chest colds and sore throats
- Gum inflammation
- Various skin issues
- Menstrual pain
- Anxiety
- Insomnia
- Stress
- Poor self-esteem
- Eating disorders

According to research released by Mount Sinai Hospital, most people in the United States, for example, who use Chamomile do so to relieve anxiety or insomnia. However wonderful, Chamomile is, there are at least eight precautions you should consider:

- Asthmatics should avoid Chamomile because it may worsen the condition
- Pregnant women should avoid Chamomile because of the potential risk of miscarriage
- Because Chamomile may act like estrogen, women who are hormone-sensitive or who have breast or uterine cancer should check with their medical doctor before using it.
- Consumption of large quantities of Chamomile tea may result in vomiting and subsequent dehydration
- Do not drive an automobile or other motorized equipment after drinking Chamomile tea
- If you are taking anticoagulants and or antiplatelets, Chamomile may increase blood thinning and potential serious bleeding if injured
- If you are taking Dilantin, Barbiturates, Xanax, or Valium check with your medical doctor because Chamomile may increase the strength of these drugs
- Chamomile may interfere with diabetes medication, hormonal therapies, and or birth control pills.

Despite these cautions, Chamomile and Chamomile tea have many positive effects:

- It is suggested that Chamomile Tea targets cancer cells and prevents them from developing (See Resources for the citation information about this specific study)
- Osteoporosis may be slowed by drinking Chamomile Tea
- Diabetes may be positively impacted because it lowers blood sugar
- Reduces inflammation
- Reduces menstrual pain
- Helps one sleep
- Reduces anxiety.

Echinacea

Echinacea is the dried root and other plant parts of any of the three purple coneflowers that are primarily used in herbal remedies. It is one of the most popular herbs used for medicinal purposes in the United States. There is anthropological evidence that Native Americans used this plant more than 400 years ago as a treatment for infections and wounds. It is an excellent caffeine-free drink.

As a rule of thumb people who have allergies or pregnant women and women who are nursing should avoid using Echinacea Tea. There are several benefits to drinking Echinacea Tea:

- Boosts immunity
- Fights the common cold
- Fights yeasts infections

- Fights Urinary Tract infection
- Relieves pain
- Soothes respiratory issues
- Releases dopamine

Ginger

As a flowering plant, Ginger is widely used for food seasoning as well as medicinal purposes. This perennial plant is closely related to three other species; Turmeric, Cardamom, and Galangal. The root of the Ginger plant is commonly used and can be fresh, dried, powdered, or as an essential oil. If you prefer to use fresh Ginger an easy way to peel it is to use a spoon and scrape off the outer layer of thin skin. It is acceptable to shred the whole root if you first rinse it off and then dry it.

Ginger has many health benefits. Here are a few:

- Brain function appears to be enhanced
- Fights infections caused by various bacteria
- May prevent cancer
- Lowers LDL
- Helps stop chronic indigestion

Hibiscus

Native to Africa and other subtropical regions of the world, Hibiscus is a species of flowering plant in the mallow family and holds a special place in many gardens around the world. Hibiscus has many benefits when made into tea. Among the more important benefits are:

- Helps destroy free radicals within your body
- Fights inflammation which plays a role in asthma and Alzheimer's Disease
- Lowers blood pressure
- Lowers cholesterol
- Supports liver health
- Helps cancer prevention

There are some cautionary notes; for example, people may be allergic to Hibiscus flowers and should avoid drinking Hibiscus Tea. There is the potentiality of a significant drop in blood pressure If you take medication for that. The same caution holds for those who suffer from diabetes.

Lemon Balm

Grown worldwide, Lemon Balm is used as an herb for seasoning, as a plant to attract bees, for medicine, cosmetics, and even for furniture polish. It's a member of the mint family. For hundreds of years, Lemon Balm has been used to reduce stress, and anxiety, improve appetite, reduce the discomfort of indigestion, and promote sleep. Additional uses for Lemon Balm include the following:

- Cold sores
- Herpes
- Listeria
- Staphylococcus

- Decreases agitation caused by Alzheimer's Disease

Passionflower

Native to the Southwestern United States and Central and South America, the Passionflower is a climbing vine with white and purple flowers. It is claimed to help the following:

- Insomnia
- Stress
- Anxiety
- ADHD
- Pain

Passionflower increases the GABA in the brain. GABA is a neurotransmitter that relaxes the central nervous system; thus, creating a positive mood and a sense of well-being. There are some restrictions. The following should avoid using Passionflower:

- Pregnant and breast-feeding women
- Very young children
- People taking sedatives
- People with allergies

The last herb for consideration is Peppermint.

Peppermint

Peppermint is a cross between spearmint and watermint. It has been used for thousands of years for health purposes. And it has been used in candies, breath mints, air fresheners, and of course tea. As with other herbs, there has not been a great deal of research to determine the exact benefits of

Peppermint use. However, some scientific studies do support its use for the following:

- Digestive issues
- Headaches and Migraines
- Breath issues
- Clogged uses
- Relieve fatigue
- Relieve menstrual cramps
- Bacterial infections
- Improve concentration.

CHAPTER THREE
TEN TEA RECIPES FOR YOUR HEALTH AND PLEASURE

"Better to be deprived of food for three days, than tea for one."
Ancient Chinese proverb

Herbal Recipe #1 Kava-kava Tea

This tea is cold. Don't even use warm water. You can use the root or powder. This recipe is for powder. Kava-kava root powder can most likely be purchased at a health food store or at a place that sells organics. This tea is for anxiety. Don't adjust this recipe. It is powerful.

Directions For one cup:

1. Measure 3 to 4 tablespoons of powder
2. Add the kava powder to a strainer or make a tea bag. Whichever one you use, but sure to secure it tightly
3. Place the bag into a large enough bowl to hold one full cup of water and to give you room to kneed the tea bag
4. Add room-temperature water
5. Let the tied bag remain at room temperature water for 5 minutes
6. Knead the tea bag with your hands for another 5 minutes. Take care that none of the kava-kava powder escapes from the bag.
7. Leave the bag in the water for another five minutes

8. Carefully pour the tea into a cup or glass and refrigerate for 20 minutes.

9. Remember this kava-kava is a hot pepper. Drink it carefully and slowly.

Herbal Recipe #2 Echinacea Tea

Ingredients:

1 to 2 tablespoons of dried Echinacea or add one teaspoon to the two for a stronger brew.

10 to 12 ounces of water

Sweetener if desired (raw honey or raw sugar)

Directions:

1. Bring the water to boil in a pot or tea kettle, or microwave

2. Pour the hot water into a cup,

3. Add the Echinacea

4. Steep for about 10 minutes

5. Remove Echinacea

6. Add sweetener (Raw Honey)

7. Enjoy

Herbal Recipe #3 Ginger Tea

Ingredients:
2 tablespoons fresh ginger root (about 2 inches)
2 cups water

1 tablespoon of fresh lemon juice adds a nice touch (optional)
1 to 2 tablespoons honey, to taste
Directions:
1. Bring the water to a boil
2. Pour hot water into a cup
3. Add the Ginger
4. Let it steep for 5 to 8 minutes
5. Add the sweetener

Herbal Recipe #4 Chamomile Tea

Ingredients

1. A good full cup of fresh Chamomile flower petals.

2. 10 ounces of boiling water

3. 1 to 2 Peppermint leaves

4. Sweetener if desired

Directions:

1. Boil the water

2. Place the Chamomile flowers in an infuser or wrap them in cheesecloth, and tie them with a piece of string. Make sure it's tight.

3. Place the teabag in the water and let it steep for a good 5 minutes

4. Pour into a warmed cup

5. Add the Peppermint leaves

6. Let the tea rest for a couple of minutes

7. Remove the Peppermint leaves

8. Add sweetener

Herbal Recipe #5 Hibiscus Tea

Ingredients
1. 1 to 4 teaspoons of Hibiscus Flower Petals

2. 8 to 10 ounces of water
3. 1 or 2 mint leaves (optional)
4. Sweetener (Raw Honey Optional)

Directions:
Boil the water either on the stovetop or in a kettle.

1. Once boiled, place the hibiscus petals in a teapot or pitcher and cover them with water.

2. Steep for 4-5 minutes, then strain, sweeten, and enjoy.

Herbal Recipe #6 Lemon Balm Tea

Ingredients

1. Two to three tablespoons of fresh Lemon Balm Leaves
2. 8 to 10 ounces of water
3. 1 slice of fresh lemon
4. Sweetener

Directions:

1. Bring the water to a rapid boil
2. Pour into a teapot or cup
3. Add Two tablespoons of Lemon Balm Leaves (in an infuser or tea bag)
4. Let this step 4 minutes
5. Add the slice of lemon
6. Add sweetener to taste

Herbal Recipe #7 Passionflower Tea

Ingredients
1. 1 to 3 teaspoons of Passionflower dried leaves
2. 8 to 10 ounces of boiling water
3. Sweetener

Directions:
1. Bring the water to boil in a stove-top pot or teapot, or use a microwave-safe cup
2. Add the Passionflower
3. Add the Sweetener of choice
4. Let it steep for 5 minutes, stir
5. Enjoy

Herbal Recipe #8 Peppermint Tea

Ingredients
1. Two to Four tablespoons of fresh peppermint leaves
2. 8 to 10 ounces of water
3. Slice of fresh lemon or lime
4. Sweetener of choice
5. 1 or 2 teaspoons of raw honey
Directions:
1. Bring the water to boil
2. Add the peppermint leaves
3. Let this steep for 5 minutes
4. Add the slice of fresh lemon
5. Add the honey
Enjoy this stomach-soothing tea.

Herbal Recipe #9 Lavender Tea

Ingredients

1. 2 to 4 tablespoons of Lavender buds
2. 8 to 10 ounces of boiling water
3. 1 teaspoon of raw honey for sweetening (if desired)

Directions:

1. Bring the water to boil
2. Place the Lavender Buds in a tea ball, or create a tea bag
3. Add the Lavender Buds to the hot water
4. Let it steep for 10 minutes
5. Pour into your favorite cup and add the sweetener
6. Enjoy

Herbal Recipe #10 Horehound Tea

Ingredients

1. 2 to 4 cups of fresh Horehound Leaves or two tablespoons of dried Horehound Leaves

2. 4 cups of water (for more than one cup of tea) or 8 to 10 ounces for 1 cup

3. 1 to 2 teaspoons of the juice of a fresh lemon (Depending on your taste)

4. 2 tablespoons of raw honey

Directions:

1. Bring the water to a boil (Adjust the amount according to the number of cups)

2. Place the leaves in a tea ball or homemade tea bag

3. Pour the water into a pre-warmed teapot

4. Add the Horehound Leaves to the teapot
5. Add the lemon juice
6. Add the honey
7. Let it steep for 5 minutes

CHAPTER FOUR
USING HERBS FOR PAIN

It is almost an understatement to say that for thousands of years herbs have been used to relieve pain. Hippocrates, the father of the Hippocratic Oath, recommended the use of what we now call aspirin for pain.

It is not within the range and scope of this course to address all the types or kinds of pain that people experience. Therefore, a select few types of pain and the suggested herbs to treat them will be included. Among the types of pain to be presented are the following:

- Migraine
- Arthritis
- Stomach
- Backpain
- Feet

Further, it is not our intent to discuss the causes of pain. You should always check with your medical doctor before using any of the suggested herbs.

Migraine Headaches
Approximately 35 million Americans suffer from migraine headaches, the majority being aged 35-45. It is estimated that 1 billion people worldwide suffer

migraines and this makes it the third most common illness in the world. And it is the sixth most disabling disease in the world. People can't work and children can't go to school because of nausea, vomiting, dizziness, and light and sound sensitivity. A billion dollars a year is spent on brain scans. You can see why it is the first pain we have chosen to deal with. The following herbs have been used to relieve migraine headaches and non-migraine headaches:

> Feverfew
> Dong Quai
> Butterbur
> Raw potato
> Peppermint
> Horseradish
> Willow Bark
> Honeysuckle
> Ginger
> Mullein
> Caffeine
> Yarrow
> Coriander
> Teaberry
> Boswellia
> Common Hopps
> Rosemary
> Betony
> Basswood
> Evodia

<u>Warning:</u> Many herbs are generally safe but they can have negative side effects. They may interfere with prescription drugs for heart issues, blood, kidney, and allergies.

Not all of these suggested herbs will be discussed. Also please note that not all of these herbs have scientific and medical studies to support claims for their use. Feverfew, Butterbur, Honeysuckle, Teaberry, and Boswellia will be examples.

<u>Feverfew,</u> as far as we currently know, was first used in the 5th Century BC in Ancient Greece. During that time, it was used for a variety of pains including headaches. Generally, one uses Feverfew dried leaves to make tea. Its use may cause bloating, canker sores, and nausea. Furthermore, it is not recommended for pregnant women, those who are on blood thinners, and those who suffer from allergies.

<u>Butterbur,</u> like other herbs, has been used throughout history. Its purified root extract appears to be the most popular created product. Purified is the operative word. If this plant is not carefully purified problems could occur. There are potentially harmful components called pyrrolizidine alkaloids. Some species of Butterbur contain two important chemicals that seem to help relieve migraine headaches: petasin and isopetasin.

<u>Honeysuckle</u> is one of the most widely used herbs in Chinese medicine and is used as an antiviral, immunomodulator, anti-inflammatory, hepatoprotectant, and neuroprotectant. The

Honeysuckle's leaves, flowers, and stems appear to be effective in reducing migraine pain. Made as a tea with a bit of raw honey, it brings temporary relief. Be careful not to confuse honeysuckle with other plants such as American ivy, gelsemium, and Clematis virginiana.

Teaberry also known as wintergreen is an edible plant. It is known for its anti-inflammatory properties and is, therefore, useful in lessening the pain of migraine headaches. Simply chop fresh leaves or use dried leaves and make tea.

Boswellia may be more familiar to you as Frankincense. Its resin is turned into tinctures, and pills, or may be used as a topical treatment. Because of the potential allergic reaction, it is recommended that a patch test be used before applying Boswellia directly to the skin. Consider mixing Boswellia with a base oil such as jojoba. Apply a small amount to each temple and between the eyebrows.

Arthritis

Some health authorities list several kinds of arthritis:

- Osteoarthritis.
- Rheumatoid arthritis.
- Spondyloarthropathies.
- Lupus erythematosus
- Gout.
- Infectious and reactive arthritis.
- Psoriatic arthritis.

The intent here is not to deal with each of these types of arthritis but to deal with this often-debilitating disease in general terms. The Arthritis Foundation suggests the following five ways to take herbs for arthritis:

- Pills and Capsules
- Infusions and Teas
- Creams, gels, and lotions
- Liquids, Extracts, and Tinctures
- Herbs for Cooking

The herbs suggested for the relief of arthritic pain include:

- Aloe Vera
- Boswellia
- Cat's Claw
- Eucalyptus
- Ginger
- Green Tea
- Thunder god Vine
- Turmeric
- Willow Bark

Of these suggested 9 herbs, only the following will be presented: Aloe Vera, Cat's claw, and Thunder god vine.

<u>Aloe Vera</u> probably is one of the most used herbs as a supportive medicine because it is readily available in several forms: pills, powder, gel, liquid, leaf, and as a live plant. Unlike the commonly used drugs for the treatment of arthritis, Aloe Vera

doesn't create gastrointestinal problems. If you choose to take Aloe Vera by mouth, be sure you DO NOT buy the juice as in 'fruit juice'. It's not as effective. Consider the following:

1. Using a live Aloe Vera plant, cut off a piece of leaf, gently squeeze the end of the cut leaf and rub it around your elbow, wrist, knee, back, or wherever you are experiencing arthritic pain.

2. Dink 2 ounces of Aloe Vera twice a day

3. Create a wrap by using cheesecloth and smashed Aloe Vera. Gently wrap it around the area in pain.

Cat's Claw comes from South and Central America and is an anti-inflammatory herb. As such, it may reduce the painful swelling caused by Arthritis, especially in your joints. It gets its name from the claw-like horns that grow along its woody vine. The effectiveness of the plant's bark and root depends on what time of year it was harvested. Cat's Claw comes in crushed, extract, capsule, and tea forms.

The World Health Organization suggests the daily dosage for each of the following forms of Cat's Claw:

• Dried stem bark extract 20=350 mg

• Capsules 300-500 mg taken two to three times a day

As with any of the suggested herbs always check with your medical doctor. There may be triggered side effects with other herbs and medicines. Some users of Cat's Claw have experienced these side effects:

- Dizziness,
- Nausea
- Diarrhea

Negative interactions may occur when using Cat's Claw with medications that suppress your immune system, blood thinners, diuretics, and blood pressure.

Thunder god vine has long been used by Chinese, Japanese, and Korean cultures for many years. I do not recommend that you create Thunder god vine extract. Extracts created from the wrong part of this herb could cause serious health issues. It could be deadly. It can create the following health issues:

- Stomach problems
- Respiratory infections
- Hair and skin damage
- Menstrual changes
- Prolonged use could lead to bone density reduction

Thunder god vine can be taken by mouth or applied to the skin and it does seem to relieve joint pain, reduce swelling, and enhance physical function in those who suffer from arthritis.

Stomach & Digestive Issues

The figures are staggering. Sixty-two million Americans are diagnosed with a digestive disorder. 20,000,000 suffer from chronic digestive issues. Further digestive disorders are one of the most prevalent causes of disability in the workforce. Twenty-five percent of the people in the United States experience indigestion yearly.

We will discuss only three herbs for stomach and/or digestive issues: Fennel, Holy Basil, and Peppermint.

Fennel

Fennel is an aromatic vegetable in the same family as carrots and celery. There are two varieties of fennel: herb fennel and Florence. Herb Fennel provides seeds to make the spice; whereas, Florence Fennel is eaten as a vegetable. The health benefits of Herb Fennel include:

- Aids digestion
- Relieves menstrual Cramps
- Relieves Colic
- Doesn't increase blood sugar because of its sweet taste

There are a couple of cautionary notes in terms of the use of fennel:

- Breastfeeding mothers should not overconsume fennel. There have been indications that doing so causes pain in the infant

- Fennel can negatively interact with medications, especially those used for seizures.

Holy Basil

Imagine being able to tackle stress, anxiety, and inflammation with a relaxing cup of tea made with the leaves of holy basil, the herb with a dozen other names.

Because of its anti-inflammatory and antioxidant properties, Holy Basil helps relieve pain for people who suffer from arthritis or fibromyalgia.

Holy basil provides all of these benefits as an adaptogen with anti-inflammatory and antioxidant properties.

There are cautionary notes in terms of the use of Holy basil:

- It may cause nausea
- If you are trying to conceive avoid Holy Basil tea
- If you are planning surgery do not drink Holy Basil Tea at least two weeks before the scheduled surgery
- It may cause drowsiness. Avoid drinking Holy Basil Tea if you are taking any medications that are designed to relax and or calm you. Avoid driving any motorized machinery including automobiles.

The use of Holy Basil tea may cause mild nausea. If you are trying to conceive it is suggested

43

that you avoid Holy basil. Holy Basil may cause slow blood clotting and it is strongly recommended that you do not drink Holy Basil Tea at least two weeks before surgery.

Peppermint

Peppermint has been used for thousands of years. Today it is used in breath mints, candies, and other foods and tea. It is said that Peppermint helps the following:
- Relaxes the digestive system
- Prevents muscles from contracting
- Relieves gut spasms
- Relieves irritable bowel syndrome
- Reduces nausea and vomiting
- Helps relieve headaches

Back Pain

Back pain afflicts 65 million every year. It may be caused by stress, physical injury, disease, poor posture, and or work. Several herbs can be used to help relieve back pain. The following three will be considered here:
- Arnica
- Bromelain
- Devil's Claw

Arnica

Arnica is a perennial plant that grows one to two feet with yellow-orange flowers very much like daisies. It's native to the mountain areas of Europe and Siberia and is cultivated in North America. Arnica has been medicinally used since the 1500s and is topically used for a wide range of conditions including:

- Back Pain
- Muscle aches
- Sprains
- Joint Pain

As an herb, Arnica is usually applied on the skin because it can have serious side effects if taken orally. Homeopathic remedies do contain Arnica but it is diluted so that it is not dangerous. Follow the directions that come with this over-the=counter medication. It's available as topical creams, and ointments as well as essential oils which can be used as the base for compresses and poultices.

Generally safe, Arnica could irritate your skin causing peeling and or blisters. Avoid using Arnica on skin that is broken. As always, pregnant women should check with their doctor before applying Arnica in any form.

For those who wish to make their own Arnica spray follow this simple recipe:

- 2 tablespoons of dried Arnica
- 6 oz of boiling water
- Add the dried Arnica to a glass jar, then carefully add the boiling water. Place the lid on the jar and let the mixture steep for a good ten minutes.
- When the liquid is completely cooled, add it to a spray bottle, and when

needed spray your skin with a couple of squirts.

If you prefer to use a salve follow this easy recipe.

- Boil one cup of water in a sterilized pot
- Once the water is at a full boil, add the following ingredients: 2 tablespoons of arnica essential oil and 1 round of beeswax. Remove the pot from the heat and let it rest for about 5 minutes.
- Add one ounce of Aloe Vera and Lavender Essential Oil (Use Rose Essential Oil if you prefer).
- Mix well. Pour into a sterilized small container that has a lid.
- I suggest placing this into a refrigerator. It makes a wonderful and refreshing rub.

Foot Pain

The old saying "when your feet hurt, you hurt all over," has much truth. The following herbs are suggested for foot soaks Peppermint Leaf, Rose Petals, Lavender Flowers, Lemon Balm, Chamomile Flowers, Holy Basil, and Rosemary.

Before using any of these suggested herbs for foot soaks be sure to check with your doctor. Sometimes negative reactions can be caused by the use of herbs.

Foot Soak #1

Ingredients:

- 1 cup of Lavender chopped
- 1 cup of Peppermint Leaves chopped
- ½ to 1 gallon of hot water

Directions:

- In a large bowl, thoroughly mix the Lavender and Peppermint
- Bring the water to a full boil; remove it from the heat and
- Add the Lavender and Peppermint mixture, stir
- Pour this mixture into a basin large enough for both of your feet.
- Test to make sure it is not too hot, place your feet in the basin, sit back and enjoy.

Foot Soak #2

Ingredients:

2 tablespoons of Fresh Rosemary chopped

2 tablespoons of Lemon Balm

2 Quarts of hot water

Directions:

Mix the two herbs and place them in a basin with hot water. When the water temperature is comfortable, soak your feet for 15 minutes.

You can use any combination of the suggested herbs. If you prefer you can use essential oils. More will be said about essential oils and healing in another course.

CHAPTER FIVE
HERBS AND ANXIETY

At some point in their lives, everyone probably experiences anxiety. An estimated 18 percent of Americans have an anxiety disorder. What is even more surprising is that only about 37% receive treatment. There are, however, those whose anxiety is so intense and prolonged that they cannot function. They may suffer severe panic attacks. Loss of job, friends, and social life may result. There are several types of anxiety disorders. Among these are the following:

- Generalized anxiety
- Social anxiety
- Separation anxiety

One may experience all of these. What then, are the signs or symptoms of anxiety? Here are a few of the common signs or symptoms:

- Nervousness
- Increased heart rate
- Rapid breathing
- Sweating
- Trembling
- Feeling weak and tired
- Trouble sleeping
- Problem concentrating

There are several types of anxiety disorders. Here are five of the more common anxiety disorders:

- Agoraphobia
- Panic Disorder
- Separation Disorder
- Social Disorder
- Drug-Induced

The causes of anxiety, like many things about the human condition, are not completely understood. Because they are not, this class is not an attempt to provide you with a medical, self-diagnostic, or self-treatment regimen. The reason people prefer natural herb remedies over prescription drugs is because of beta-blockers. For whatever reason, you choose to use herbal remedies CONSULT your MEDICAL DOCTOR.

Due diligence is always appropriate. For quite some time Kava seemed to be an appropriate treatment for anxiety. However, it was soon found that even short-term use of Kava caused serious liver damage. As a consequence, the United States Food and Drug Administration issued a warning about dietary supplements containing Kava.

Remember some herbs can negatively interact with over-the-counter medicines as well as with prescription medicine. They can increase or decrease the effects of drugs and cause potentially serious health issues.

The following herbs will be considered for use in the relief of anxiety:

- Ashwagandha
- Chamomile
- Lavender
- Hops
- Lemon Balm
- St. John's Wort

ASHWAGANDHA

Ashwagandha also known as winter cherry is an evergreen shrub. It is grown in India, the Middle East, and parts of Africa. It has been used for thousands of years to improve one's concentration and to increase one's energy level, it is best known for its stress-relieving properties. And that includes anxiety.

The yellow flowers and roots are used to make extracts and powders. It is classified as an adaptogen because it helps the body cope with stress and its resulting anxiety. It is suggested that 500–600 mg of ashwagandha per day for 6–12 weeks may reduce anxiety and lower the likelihood of insomnia in people with stress and anxiety disorders.

Avoid

Women who are pregnant should avoid using ashwagandha because it may cause the loss of the pregnancy. Those with hormone-sensitive prostate cancer should not use ashwagandha; nor those who are taking certain medications such as benzodiazepines or barbiturates. Additionally, some users have reported gastrointestinal problems, drowsiness, and diarrhea.

CHAMOMILE

Chamomile as an herbal medicine has been used for a variety of physical issues as well as emotional issues. This daisy-like flower is so widely used it is nearly synonymous with calming. It relieves anxiety. It is available as a tea, tablet, and as an extract.

One study has shown that long-term use of chamomile extracts significantly reduced GAD (Generalized Anxiety Disorder).

It is suggested that adults should take 400 to 1600 mg in capsule form in divided daily doses. One to four milligrams of liquid extract 3 times a day and Chamomile Tincture 15 milligrams 3 to 4 times daily.

Remember what works for one person may not necessarily work for you. And please remember some may experience allergic reactions. This is especially true if they have negative reactions to these plants:

- Ragweed
- Chrysanthemums
- Marigolds
- Daisies

Furthermore, Chamomile may not react well to warfarin and other blood thinners. It should not be taken if you are using the antirejection drug, cyclosporine.

It is imperative that you check with your medical doctor before using any natural remedies.

LAVENDER

The earliest recorded use of lavender dates back to ancient Egypt where it played a role in the mummification processes, Lavender was used as a bath additive in ancient Persia, Greece, and Rome. These early cultures believed that lavender helped purify the body and mind. Today Lavender is available as sprays, perfumes, disinfectants, air fresheners, and essential oil. Besides these everyday uses, Lavender has value as a medicinal herb. It is especially helpful to those who suffer from anxiety. There are two distinct approaches to using Lavender for anxiety. These are

- Oral
- Aromatherapy
- Massage

The most effective way to make use of Lavender orally is to take a capsule. Some human usage studies have suggested that Lavender Capsules are the most effective with a daily dose of 80 to 160 mg per day.

As aromatherapy, Lavender is an effective treatment to be used in one's home office, in the bedroom, or in other living spaces. Using a good diffuser, and following its directions, be sure you use pure Lavender Essential Oil.

As a massage, you can apply Lavender Essential Oil directly to the skin. However, make sure you do not have issues if it is applied directly to the skin. Do a small patch test. You can also add pure oil to a base oil such as jojoba. If you have a sudden anxiety attack, gently rub one or two drops on your temples.

If you experience anxiety attacks while in a public situation you can carry a small roll-on bottle of Lavender Essential Oil with you. Apply it to the back of your wrists.

HOPS

The term "hops" comes from the Anglo-Saxon term "hoppan", which means "to climb. Hops are green cone-shaped climbing perennial flowers. Its fame lies in the creation of beer but despite that particular fame, it is also an excellent aid in dealing with anxiety.

Hops are probably safe when used short term. Suggested doses of up to 300 mg daily for 3 months. However, the appropriate dose of hops depends on several factors:

- User's age
- User's health
- Users' sensitivity

 Always check with your medical doctor.

Pregnant and breastfeeding women should avoid using hops. Depression could worsen using hops. Those who have hormone-sensitive cancers should not use hops. Persons having surgery should not use hops for at least two weeks before the surgery. It might interfere with the anesthesia.

LEMON BALM

A member of the mind family, lemon balm is considered to be a calming herb. The history of its use dates hundreds of years and included the use for stress, anxiety, and to improve appetite. To lift the spirits, it was steeped in wine. Additionally, it combines well with other herbs.

Lemon Balm can be used fresh or dried and it is available as tea, supplement pills, and essential oil. There are several varieties of lemon balm. Among these are:

- Aurea
- All gold
- Citronella
- Lemonella

It is believed that lemon balm inhibits certain brain chemicals thus boosting calmness.

Here are a half dozen preparation methods and suggested uses:

- Tea
- Food
- Capsules
- Tinctures
- Extract
- Aromatherapy

You should not use lemon balm if you are pregnant, breastfeeding, have a history of seizures, or if surgery is scheduled. It is questionable if it's suitable for children. As a consequence, I do not recommend giving Lemon Balm in any form to children.

ST. JOHN'S WORT

St. John's Wort is a yellow-flowered plant that is one of the top-selling supplements in the United States. It is believed that this natural plant works by keeping the brain from using up important neurotransmitters such as serotonin and dopamine. This has an antidepressant effect which results in fewer bouts of anxiety.

Using a pill (capsule or tablet) the dosage for mild anxiety is suggested to be 300 mg 3 times a day with meals. It is also available as an extract and as a tea. Consult your medical doctor to help with the dosage of the extract or amount of tea you should drink daily.

The use of St. John's Wort may cause dizziness, dry mouth, fatigue, sensitivity to sunlight, and upset stomach and may induce metabolization of certain medications such as birth control pills, and medicine used for HIV treatment.

As with all the suggested use of herbs included in this course, please check with your medical doctor. And do so, especially if you are taking any medications.

CHAPTER SIX
HERBS FOR SKIN AND HAIR

Skincare is an important part of hygiene. On a global level, consumers spend an estimated $382 billion on cosmetics. In 2021, skincare products rose to $135 billion globally. With that amount of money being spent annually one has to ask are these products safe. How are cosmetics defined? Are they different from skincare products?

The United States Federal Food, Drug, and Cosmetic Act define cosmetics by their intended use: rubbed, poured, sprinkled, or sprayed on. It then identifies purposes for use such as cleaning, beautifying, promoting attractiveness, or altering the appearance.

But the FD&C Act does not end there. It lists the types of products: skin moisturizers, perfumes, lipsticks, fingernail polishes, eye, and facial makeup, and cleansing shampoos.

A simple definition of cosmetics is a product that temporarily changes your physical appearance. For our purposes here, skincare is defined as any product dealing with specific skin issues. The technical name for these products is *cosmeceuticals*. Even though cosmetics and cosmeceuticals deal with problems related to how one looks, there are some differences. Among these differences are the following:

- Cosmetics are a temporary fix; whereas, skincare products treat the root cause of a skin concern and aim for a permanent positive result.

- Cosmetics result in an immediate fix for a problem

- Dermatologists and Skincare professionals generally do not recommend cosmetics

- Cosmetics do not have the purpose of healing; whereas, skincare products do,

- Cosmeceuticals are formulated with skin problems as the focus

- Cosmetics are available in grocery stores, health stores, and online. Cosmeceuticals are not.

Before I go into which herbs do what, I want to address another aspect of skincare: the toxic chemicals and contaminants found in cosmetics. The area of cosmetics and skincare are not subjected to a lot of government regulations. The following carcinogens and chemicals are in many cosmetic and skincare products and are considered cancer-causing:

- Formaldehyde is intentionally added to products that are designed for hair straightening, nail polish, eye shadow, and mascara

- Phenacetin is used as a stabilizer in facial hair bleach, and hair color
- Coal Tar is used in hair dyes, shampoos, dandruff treatment, and rosacea treatment
- Benzene is sometimes used in hair conditioners and styling lotions
- Mineral Oils are in many personal care items such as eye shadow, moisturizers, blush, and concealers
- Ethylene Oxide is found in personal care products

Always read the labels of any cosmetic and skincare products before purchasing and using them.

An alternative to chemically loaded hair and skin care products is herbs. Just to remind you, an herb is a plant with aromatic qualities whose leaves and stems are used for food seasonings as well as medicinal purposes. We also include other parts of a plant such as roots, berries, seeds, twigs, needles, and bark. Herbal application may be in the form of a liquid, cream, ointment, or paste.

For our purposes here, the following herbs for skin care will be considered:

- Aloe Vera
- Chamomile
- Sage
- Mint
- Oat Straw
- Basil

- Horsetail
- Calendula

Always check with your medical doctor before beginning the use of any of the herbs suggested.

loe Vera

Aloe Vera is a cactus-like plant. It is grown in dry and hot climates. It has long been used for wound healing, skin conditions, and hair issues. It can be used topically and orally. Topical use includes the following:

Acne
Skin Rashes
Burns
Herpes Simplex

Aloe Vera plants are a good idea to keep in your home. They are easy to care for. Simply water aloe vera plants deeply, but infrequently. Make sure you do not overwater. Allow the top third of the potting soil to dry out between waterings.

Aloe Vera is available as a liquid and as a juice. We will revisit this wonderful healing plant when we talk about hair care.

Chamomile

We devoted a considerable amount of time to this multi-use herb in the section about teas. Because it is high in the compound, alpha-bisabolol, Chamomile soothes acne, rashes, and eczema. It reduces the discoloration of the skin caused by sunburns or acne.

Using either fresh or dried Chamomile leaves, brew 24 ounces of tea, and let it completely cool. Wash your face in the tea to help reduce the fine lines and wrinkles

Make a teabag from cheesecloth, fill it with Chamomile, place it in boiling water, remove the teabag, let the teabag cool until it is just warm, and place it over your eyes to remove puffiness and or dark circles. Leave the teabags on your eyes for about 5 minutes.

Sage

Sage is a powerful antioxidant and because it is, it is anti-aging. It fights free radicals and is an astringent for oily skin. It helps control acne. An added plus to the use of sage is that it is rich in two important vitamins: A and calcium both play a significant role in cell regeneration.

To make a facial wash boil 8 to 10 cups of water. (If you are a purist, don't use tap water.) Add 4 teaspoons of sage powder or 6 teaspoons of fresh chopped sage leaves. Let this steep for 10 minutes. Gently wash your face and pat dry. Do this daily. You can make enough tea for a week if it's refrigerated.

Mint

Mint is an excellent treatment for acne, pimples, and oily skin. It will soothe itchy skin as well. Mint leaves contain salicylic acid and Vitamin A which help control sebum secretions, the culprit in many skin issues. Sebum is essential for healthy skin but sometimes the skin produces too much. It clogs pores, and they become inflamed.

Mint helps heal cuts, minor wounds, insect bites, and itchy sunburned skin. To treat acne, you will need the following:

Ingredients
- 15 to 20 fresh mint leaves
- 1 tablespoon of crushed oats
- 1 fresh cucumber juiced (Make sure you get at least 1 to 1 ½ tablespoons of juice)
- 1 teaspoon of raw honey

Directions:
- Add all the ingredients to a mixing bowl
- Blend the ingredients until a smooth thick paste formed
- Apply the paste to the acne, cut, or itchy skin
- Leave the paste on for 15 minutes; rinse with warm water

Additional benefits of Mint Leaves include the following:
- Hydrates the skin
- Slows aging
- Reduces dark circles
- Brightens your complexion

Oat Straw

Oat Straw is a cereal grass that comes from the stems of the unripened *Avena sativa Plant.* The stems release a milky sap. This can be added to complement the tea to create a stronger and perhaps more effective infusion. Follow these directions to make one cup of Oat Straw Infusion:

- Two cups of water
- 2 to 3 teaspoons of dried Oat Straw
- Bring the water to boil
- Pour the boiling water over the Oat Straw
- Let it steep for 15 to 20 minutes

When it is cool enough, gently wash your face. It is suggested to wash your face in the morning and again before retiring.

Because research on its safety is sketchy, it is not recommended for pregnant women or young children.

Basil

Basil's properties are antiseptic and because they are it can be used to treat several skin conditions. The juice of the Basil plant topically used can help improve skin issues caused by fungal infections and even ringworm. Basil helps tighten your skin pores. Well known as an anti-aging herb, Basil helps rejuvenate the skin. Here are the directions for making a Basil face mask:

- 1 to 2 bunches of fresh Basil

- Thoroughly wash the Basil and pat dry with a clean towel
- Place the Basil in a stainless-steel bowl
- Using a stainless-steel chopper, chop the Basil into very fine pieces
- Using a sterilized wooden spoon, smash the Basil into a pulp
- Add one or two tablespoons of jojoba base oil, and mix until a smooth paste forms
- If you prefer add one to two drops of Rose or Lavender Oil
- Clean your face, dry, and apply the Basil paste.
- Leave on your face until the paste is semi-dry, rinse and pat dry.
- Do this three times a week.

Before you apply this Basi Mask to your face, do a small patch test. If any redness appears check with your medical doctor before using.

Horsetail

Horsetail goes by several names including bottle brush. It contains silicon, a trace mineral the body uses for flexible joints, strong bones, and great skin. Horsetail has been around for more than 100 million years. The stem looks like asparagus. It gradually withers as it turns brown. Its stems turn green and are very thin and hairlike, thus its name, Horsetail.

It has been used as a diuretic, to increase blood circulation, ease the pain of arthritis, and treat ulcers. As true as that is, our interest here is in the silicon it contains. The silica and silica acids are more prevalent in Horsetail than in other herbs.

Before I continue a note of significant clarification: Silicon and Silicone. Silicone, first of all, is man-made, and second, it is used in a variety of industrial projects.

To make a horsetail extract, the leaves of the horsetail plant are harvested at a particular point in their life cycle and dried.

The leaves are then steeped in boiling water which forms a type of tea that you can drink. Highly concentrated Horsetail "tea" becomes a Horsetail Extract that you can use in base oils for your skincare. Some of the benefits of Horsetail for the skin include:

- Tighter and firmer look to your skin
- Tones the look of your skin
- Skin texture is improved
- Skin moisture improved

Horsetail comes in powders, cut leaves, and tinctures. Make sure that whatever source of purchase you use, is reliable. Follow the directions that come with the order. But make sure you make enough to last a month. Gently wash your face, neck, and hands with the Horsetail tea.

Calendula

Calendula is a flowering plant that has bright yellow or vibrant orange petals. It is a member of the same family as Marigolds, Dahlias, Chrysanthemums, and Chamomiles. It grows to about 2 feet in height and can be grown in most places throughout the world. Calendula helps you to keep your skin moisturized, slow skin aging, and heal skin issues use.

To use Calendula, make a tea and gently apply it to the skin. You can use a soft cloth or your hands to apply the Calendula tea to your skin.

Or consider a mask made of Calendula and carrier oil. Test the mask before leaving it on your face for the full 15 minutes. If it irritates you in any way remove the mask, and refrain from using it until you consult your medical doctor.

CHAPTER SEVEN
HERBS AND HAIR

The estimated expenditure of hair salons for 2022 is more than $46 billion. Global hair and scalp care in 2021 was over $80 billion. An additional $8 billion was spent on natural hair care products. These figures are expected to increase considerably now that it is becoming acceptable for men to use hair care products.

The Food and Drug Administration of the United States does not review what it considers to be personal care products. And that includes hair products with one exception, color additives. Consequently, harmful chemicals can show up in the products you use for personal care, especially hair products.

Your first line of defense is to read the labels. The highest concentration of an ingredient is listed first. Second, don't fall for the celebratory promotion of new products.

Here is a list of 7 chemicals to not have in the hair products you use:

- Formaldehyde is known to cause eye and skin issues, lung problems, and immunotoxicity.

- Parabens can interfere with human sexual hormone production resulting in reproductive problems in men and women

- Phthalates, used in shampoos, conditioners, hairsprays, and fragrances. They can cause low sperm count in males and infertility in women.

- Sodium Lauryl Sulfate is the main ingredient in shampoos. It's what makes the shampoo lather. It is also the top chemical to avoid in hair products. Linked to kidney, liver, and central nervous issues.

- Propylene Glycol provides a shiny appearance to your hair but it can also create skin irritation

- Polyethylene Glycol, used to deep clean your hair, contains Ethylene Oxide a possible carcinogen.

- Mineral Oil contains polyaromatic hydrocarbons that are linked to nonmelanoma skin cancer.

The question is what can you do about the use of harmful chemicals? Read the labels. If you don't know what something is, take the time to look it up. Of course, complain to the manufacturers as well as government agencies. There are three apps you can use to help find non-toxic products. Check References for the URLs for these apps.

The old saying "you can't go home again" doesn't apply to the resurgent use of nature-based products. You can revisit those herbs of bygone days to create safe hair care for today.

The following herbs are recommended for hair are:

- Aloe Vera
- Saw Palmetto
- Gingko Biloba
- Ginseng
- Burdock
- Coat Buttons
- Rosemary
- Brahmi
- Stinging Nettle
- Gooseberry

Aloe Vera

Aloe vera's thick leaves contain a gel-like substance. Cut off a piece of the Aloe Vera plant leaf and gently rub its liquid into the scalp. Let it penetrate your hair follicles to condition and improve damaged, dry hair. Let it sit for 60 minutes then wash your hair with a mild chemically safe shampoo.

If you choose not to use the live plant gel Aloe Vera Gel can be purchased from health product stores or online.

Ginkgo Biloba

Ginkgo Biloba is also known as silver apricot and is said to live for 1500 years. It is claimed that 40% of women show visible signs of hair loss by the time they are in their 40s. The University of Maryland Medical Center in 2020 advised using a Gingko Biloba extract for alopecia and other hair issues. The recommended dosage is 40 to 80 mg 3 times a day. The improvement in blood circulation helps the hair grow. Ginko as it is commonly called can help the hair in the following ways:

- Increase blood flow to the scalp
- Nourishes damaged hair follicles
- Increase and maintains micro capillary circulation
- Supports the healing of an inflamed scalp

Burdock

Used for hundreds of years for digestive issues has since 2010 made a significant comeback as a medicinal herb. It has been demonstrated that the root has powerful antioxidants which protect the body from damage caused by free radicals.

The root of the Burdock may be brown or black and it is the root that holds many benefits for human hair and scalp. Among these benefits are the following:

- Promotes hair growth
- Builds hair proteins
- Soothes and calms scalp irritation
- Nourishes the scalp
- Combats Folliculitis

You should take ½ teaspoon (1,200 milligrams) of Burdock Powder once or twice a day. Or the dosage as instructed by your physician. It's best to take the supplement with meals.

Rosemary

Rosemary certainly is one of the more recognizable plants. Its popularity goes well beyond food seasoning. Rosemary's use for hair includes the following:

- Hair Growth
- Hear Cleanser
- Restores Shine and luster
- Scalp Issues

There are several ways to use Rosemary to meet the four basic hair issues. We will present two do-it-yourself treatments for hair issues.

Creating Infused Rosemary Oil

You will need the following: 8 to 12 Fresh Rosemary stems (homegrown, local farmer's markets, or your local grocery store are great sources). Strip the Rosemary needles from the steps, rinse in fresh water, and pat dry.

You may need to wait 10 or 20 minutes to make sure the needles are dry. Once dry, use a mortar and pestle to crush the Rosemary needles. Or wrap the needles in a paper towel or wax paper, and pound them with a hammer until they are thoroughly crushed.

Carefully chose a base oil (carrier oil), making sure it is not sensitive to heat like coconut oil. Consider jojoba, olive, walnut, or macadamia oil) Jojoba is generally considered safe. If you have allergies that are nut based avoid those oils and if you are not sure do a patch test and or consult your medical doctor.

1.   Place the crushed Rosemary in a sterilized glass jar with a lid.

2.   Slowly pour your carrier oil over the Rosemary. Place the lid on the jar, making sure it is on tight.

3.   Store the jar in a cool and dark place.

4.   Leave the jar with its Rosemary in its place for about 2 weeks.

5.   Using a small amount, gently rub the Rosemary Infused Oil into your scalp, pulling it through your hair.

6.   Do this once or twice a week

As with all the suggested recipes in this course, you can alter and or modify the directions to fit your requirements.

Creating a Rosemary Rinse

Boil 8 to 10 cups of water

Add 6 to 8 springs of washed Rosemary

Let it steep for 30 minutes

Pour the mixture through a strainer to remove the Rosemary

Pour the liquid into a clean container

The Rosemary rinse can be used as a hair cleansing agent, to help restore a shine to your hair, and as a treatment for dandruff and or scalp irritation. Don't rinse. Use a towel to dry your hair.

Stinging Nettle

Generally considered safe to use, Stinging Nettle can generate negative side effects. Among these are the following:

- Stomach upset
- Fluid retention
- Sweating
- Diarrhea
- Hives
- Rash

Because Stinging Nettle may alter the menstrual cycle and may contribute to miscarriage, pregnant women should avoid its use. Furthermore, there is some indication that the oral use of Stinging Nettle may cause issues with diabetes and for those who are on blood thinners.

Despite all these precautions, Stinging Nettle is considered safe to use for the treatment of hair issues. Accordingly, the following procedures for hair loss and growth are suggested.

Creating Stinging Nettle Hair Rinse

The procedure is the same as described for creating a Rosemary Rinse. However, if you choose to make your rinse from fresh Stinging Nettle use caution if you are harvesting the Nettle. Use good quality rubber gloves. If you pick barehanded, then follow this procedure:

- Pinch the stem of the plant between your thumb and forefinger

- Select the top couple of leaves, and bring your hand, umbrella-like, down over the of top the leaves.

- Begin on the outside of a patch of Stinging Nettle, and avoid reaching over the plants to get to the next row.

You can use dried and or frozen Stinging Nettle to create the rinse. Whether you use fresh, dried, or frozen, apply the rinse once a week. You may need to adjust the number of times you apply the Stinging Nettle Rinse per week to achieve noticeable results.

Saw Palmetto

Saw Palmetto, a member of the palm family is a shrub native to the South East United States. Its yellow berries ripen to a dark black. These berries are crushed into a powder that is used in capsule and liquid form. Saw Palmetto helps prevent hair loss as well as stimulates hair growth.

If you are considering taking Saw Palmetto as a supplement, I strongly recommend you check with your medical doctor first. With that caution stated, it is generally suggested a standard dose is 320mg. Take it with food. If, however, you are applying Saw Palmetto topically, try it twice weekly. If you are taking birth control medications do not use Saw Palmetto. The same holds for anticoagulants. Here are two approaches to using Saw Palmetto to help stop hair loss and stimulate hair growth.

Saw Palmetto Rinse

You will need Aloe Vera and ground Saw Palmetto.

Mix 2 to 4 ounces of Aloe Vera with 1 tablespoon of ground Saw Palmetto. Thoroughly mix until you have a smooth paste. Gently apply to your scalp. Leave the mixture on your scalp for about 15 minutes. Rinse with tepid water. You may a mild shampoo afterward.

Creating Your Own Saw Palmetto Shampoo

You will need the following:
- ½ cup of water
- ½ cup of Castile liquid soap
- 1 tablespoon of light vegetable oil. Avocado for example.
- 3 to 5 drops of rose or lavender essential oil

Mix all the ingredients until they are smooth but not frothy. You may need to adjust the Castile soap because it is a strong soap. Men may want to consider adding cedar essential oil in place of rose or lavender essential oil.

Wet your hair, and gently rub in the shampoo until it is a good lathering. Let this stand for 5 to 10 minutes (Your preference), and rinse with mildly warm water. Pat dry with a cloth towel. Avoid using a high-powered electric hair dryer.

Ginseng

Ginseng is a slow-growing plant with medicinal benefits, including energy, treatment for colds, and hair growth. It has been an important ingredient in traditional Chinese medicine.

Because Ginseng is a natural plant and contains no harmful toxins. It fights hair loss, strengthens hair roots, and increases blood flow to the scalp.

Easy Scalp Treatment Using Ginseng
- You will need Ginseng powder.
- Jojoba Oil or one of the nut oils if you have no allergies

Directions

1 tablespoon of Ginseng Powder

4 ounces of Jojoba Oil or oil of your choice

Mix until creamy and apply to your scalp with a gentle massage for at least 5 minutes.

Let it rest for another 5 to 10 minutes. Rinse and dry hair with a soft towel.

Coat Buttons

Despite being declared a noxious weed, Coat Buttons have medicinal value. It has enjoyed a long time of use in traditional Indian medicine. Scientific studies have shown that the Coat Buttons Plant has antiviral, antibiotic, and antioxidant properties. when it comes to growing hair. If you choose to do independent research on Coat Buttons, be sure to use Coat Buttons Plant. Otherwise, you will end up with all kinds of physical buttons to sew on your coat.

Coat Button Oil for Hair Growth

This recipe calls for two to four bunches of fresh Coat Button leaves. More may be added if needed.

You will need

- A blender.
- A pan for cooking
- A spoon for stirring
- A thick piece of cheesecloth (Enough to cover the top of the glass jar)
- Essential Oil (Rose, Lavender, Cedar)
- Coconut Oil
- Light Olive Oil or Avocado Oil
- An empty sterilized glass jar with a lid
- MSM Powder

Directions

1. Gently rinse the Coat Buttons; pat dry with a paper towel or clean cloth towel.

2. Place the leaves, stems, and roots in the blender. Blend until a paste is created.

3. Add 3 to 4 tablespoons of Light Olive Oil or Avocado Oil to the cooking pan. Turn on low heat.

4. Add 1 Tablespoon of MSM Powder, and stir constantly so it doesn't stick to the bottom of the pan.

5. Add the crushed Coat Buttons to the heated oil. Stir constantly.

6. Cook until the color changes. Remove from heat.

7. Pour the contents into the cheesecloth and let the oil drain into the glass jar.

8. Once the cooked leaves are cool enough to handle, carefully lift the cheesecloth from the jar and squeeze the remaining oil into your jar.

9. Add 1 tablespoon of Coconut Oil. Add 5 drops of Essential Oil.

10. Mix thoroughly.

11. Once cool, apply to your scalp in a gentle massage.

Brahmi

First, Brahmi has several names. Bacopa is often used to mean Brahmi. Unfortunately, it is also the name of a groundcover. Brahmi is an edible herb; whereas, the groundcover, Bacopa is not. Originally a plant native to India, it is now available in other tropical regions of the world.

Brahmi is a creeping herb that grows to about 6 inches. It's a good example of a sprawling plant. Brahmi is a soft-stemmed plant with bright green oval leaves. Its flowers are small white colored with yellow centers. It can be mixed with oils. All parts of the Brahmi plant are usable and can be made into oil or powder. Applied to the scalp for improved hair, it offers several high benefits.

- Prevents split ends

- Reduces hair loss
- Eliminates dandruff,
- Prevents dry scalp
- Increases hair health

To apply Brahmi to improve your hair follow these steps:

1. In a small glass bowl, add five or six teaspoons of Brahmi Powder.
2. Add 3 tablespoons of heated Mustard Oil (Heat just long enough to warm the oil)
3. Mix the Brahmi Powder and the Mustard Oil into a smooth paste
4. Apply this to your scalp and massage well.
5. Then apply it to your hair, from root to tip.
6. Leave the paste on for 60 minutes.
7. Rinse off and then shampoo. If possible, use a sulfate-free shampoo.

Amla

Amla also known as the Indian Gooseberry Tree is grown in India and Burma. It is considered a "wonder drug" when it comes to the care of your hair. The claimed benefits of Alma use include the following:

- Hair growth
- Reduces graying of hair
- Strengthens hair follicles
  - Reduces hair thinning

Using Amla for improving your hair and stimulating hair growth and doing so in the comfort of your own home is easy. It has been recommended that Amla Hair Tonic be used 3 times a week. This suggested recipe is for a sufficient quantity for three days.

You will need the following:
- Six teaspoons of Amla Powder
- Six Tablespoons of Coconut Oil
- 3 Tablespoons of Olive Oil

Directions:
- Combine the two oils. (Coconut and Olive) in a saucepan
- Heat the oils.
- Add the Amla Powder
- Heat until it turns brown.
- Remove the pan from the heat and set it aside to cool
- Once the Amla Powder settles, collect the oil in a jar with a cap.
- While the mixture is slightly warm, massage one teaspoon into your scalp. Do this for 10 to 15 minutes. You may have to add a bit more oil.
- Work the oil through your hair.
- Wait for 20 to 30 minutes leaving the oil in your hair
- Shampoo your hair with a shampoo that has no sulfate.
- Towel dry your hair. No electric hair dryer.

A final note. Be patient, and give your selected treatment time to work. If you are experiencing hair issues don't put off treatment. The longer you wait, the longer it will take to repair the problem.

CHAPTER EIGHT
HERBS FOR FOOT PAIN

In 2020 $2.7 billion was spent on foot care products. An exact figure on the amount people spend on foot surgeries is not available right now. However, depending on the surgery, we have an estimate of the cost if you are paying out of pocket. The cost is between $4,000 and $170,000. Shamanic healing practices suggest the use of medicinal plants to help reduce uncomfortable issues with the feet.

Because of the extended stay-at-home work created by the Covid-19 pandemic, people moved into a more relaxed work ethic. Casual dress, less use of make-up, and going unshaven. These stay-at-homers also stopped wearing shoes around their homes. Two podiatrists at Cedars-Sinai have indicated that going barefoot has led to soreness and injury to the feet such as Plantar Fasciitis, Tendinitis, and Metatarsalgia.

Foot pain from being overweight, having flat feet, being on your feet long hours, diabetes, sciatica, lack of Calcium and/or Vitamin D, gout, Achilles tendonitis, and peripheral neuropathy can and do make life miserable.

Who may be at risk for foot pain?

- Middles-aged men are prone to having pain in their toes
- Young women athletes are likely to experience in the sole and dome of their feet
- Heel pain becomes an issue for women 40s to 50s who are sedentary
- Foot and nail pain impacts men over the age of 55 who are afflicted with arthritis or diabetes

Common foot pain symptoms include the following:

- Muscles, joints, and ligaments of the feet
- Soles have a burning sensation near the heal
- Swelling and numbness due to inflammation
- Pain between the big toe and second toe (the long toe)

Herbs are used in the treatment of Plantar Fasciitis, in fighting foot fungus, and in general foot pain. They are a lot less expensive than many of the over-the-counter medications currently available. The following material is suggested as supportive medicine, not a replacement for modern medical treatment. Here are four do-at-home easy recipes for relieving foot pain.

One of my favorite treatments for painful feet is Rosemary. When used as a foot bath it brings considerable pain relief.

1. ROSEMARY FOOT SOAK
   <u>What You Will Need</u>
   A pot for boiling water
   A basin large enough to soak your feet
   Fresh Rosemary
   A knife
   A towel
   Olive oil
   Water
   <u>Ingredients</u>
   4 to 5 sprigs of fresh Rosemary (dried Rosemary can be used) If you use dried Rosemary, 4 to 5 tablespoons will work

   1 tablespoon of olive oil

   4 to six cups of water
   <u>Directions</u>
   In a pot, bring the water to a rapid boil

   Chop the Rosemary into smaller pieces

   Once the water is boiling, remove from the heat and add the Rosemary sprigs.

   Add the olive oil. Slowly stir.

   Add the mixture to a pan large enough to hold your feet. Let the mixture cool until it's comfortable for you. Some may wish to remove the Rosemary sprigs.

   Sit in a chair, and place your feet in the pan containing the mixture. Soak your feet for 15 minutes. Dry with a soft towel.

   Repeat daily if necessary: Morning or evening

2. TRIPLE HERB FOOT SOAK
   <u>What You Will Need</u>
   A pot for boiling water
   A tablespoon
   A basin large enough to soak your feet
   Calendula, Lavender, and Comfrey leaves
   A towel

<u>Ingredients</u>
   4 tablespoons of dried and crushed Calendula flower buds
   3 tablespoons of dried and crushed Lavender
   3 tablespoons of dried comfrey leaves
   2 to 4 quarts of boiling water

<u>Directions</u>
   In a large bowl, mix the dry ingredients
   Once thoroughly mixed, add the boiling water and stir
   Pour into a basin large enough to hold your feet
   Test the water to make sure it is not too hot
   Soak your feet for 15 minutes. Pat dry with a soft towel

3. GINGER FOOT SOAK
   <u>What You Will Need</u>
   A pot for boiling water
   A tablespoon
   A basin large enough for your feet
   Stone pebbles
   Fresh Ginger
   Olive Oil

Clean towel

Directions

Boil enough water to cover your feet.

Grate 4 tablespoons of fresh Ginger

Add enough stone pebbles to cover the bottom of the basin

Add half of the boiled water

Add the grated ginger, stir around

Add 1 tablespoon of olive oil and stir

Add the remaining hot water

Test before placing your feet in the pan. If It's not too hot, soak your feet for 15 minutes.

Pat dry with a clean soft towel.

(You can drain the liquid from the foot pan and use it at least once more if you so choose.)

4. WILLOW BARK

What You Will Need

Enough boiled water to cover your feet

A basin large enough for both feet

A sharp knife

Tablespoon

Willow branches

Olive Oil

Essential Rose Oil

Directions

Boil enough water to cover both feet

While the water is coming to a boil, cut the bark from the Willow branches. (You may be able to buy the dried Willow Bark.)

Pour the water into your basin

Add the Willow Bark

Add 2 tablespoons of Olive Oil

Add 3 drops of Rose Essential Oil (You may choose another essential oil such as Lavender or Cedar)

Stir the water until all ingredients are mixed. Test the water to see if it is comfortable.

Soak your feet for 15 to 20 minutes

Pat dry with a soft towel

In addition to our four examples, the following herbs are also useful in relieving foot pain: Peppermint Leaf, Lemon Balm, Holy Basil, Oat Tops, and Red Clover Blossoms. The procedures suggested in making the herb foot soaks are just that—suggestions.

CHAPTER NINE
HERBS FOR BACK PAIN

Approximately 65 million Americans report some form of back pain. Sixteen million experience chronic back pain. Back pain costs over $12 million yearly. Over 80 million days of work are lost each year due to back pain. Over the past 20 years, Americans spent $134 billion on back pain remedies. One way to cut down that enormous expenditure and still get relief from back pain is to incorporate herbs into your treatment.

Continual nagging back pain can be a sign of serious physical issues and it can cause psychological problems as well. Personal relationships suffer as well as potential job loss results because of chronic back pain. These herbs are suggested as providers of pain relief: Turmeric, Solomon's Seal, Devil's Claw, Boswellia, and Ginger. Remember to check with your medical doctor if you have questions about the use of any of these herbs.

TURMERIC TEA
Boil 2 cups of water
Warm a tea cup with part of the boiled water.
Using the remaining water, fill the cup ¾ full.

Add ½ teaspoon of Turmeric Powder (You may use ground fresh Turmeric)

Add a pinch of Cayenne Pepper to speed up the absorption

Add 1 tablespoon of raw honey for flavoring.

Let it steep for 10 minutes before drinking. Sip throughout the day.

SOLOMON'S SEAL

If you are a do-it-yourself individual **use only the roots** of this plant. Other parts are poisonous and this is true especially of the berries. With that said, keep in mind that natural products are not always safe.

Making Solomon's Seal Lotion

You will need 3 tablespoons of Solomon's Seal Roots

Grind the Roots into a fine powder (You may be able to buy Solomon's Seal Root Powder)

4 to 6 ounces of carrier oil such as Jojoba Oil (Sweet Almond Oil, Olive Oil, or Avocado Oil)

Mix Solomon's Seal with the carrier oil.

Apply to the base of the spine or upper back. To give it an extra boost, slightly warm the oil before applying it.

Making Solomon's Seal Tea

You will need 8 to 14 ounces of boiling water

Add ½ teaspoon of dried Solomon's Seal Root

Let it steep for 5 to 8 minutes. The kernels of Solomon's Seal Root will puff up. By the way, you can chew the softened root.

Add 1 teaspoon of raw honey if you prefer

It is suggested you drink 3 cups a day.

If you are taking other medications, check with your doctor before using Solomon's Seal. It might interfere with those medications and negatively impact their effectiveness.

DEVIL'S CLAW

Unfortunately, other plant species are called Devil's Claw including those grown in the United States. The one that is said to have medicinal properties is gown in southern Africa. Its Latin name is Harpagophytum procumbens.

Making Devil's Claw Tea

Two cups of boiling water

Add 1 tablespoon of powdered Devil's Claw

Steep for at least 6 hours.

Strain and discard the leftover Devil's Claw

Drink 2 to 3 times a day

Making Devil's Claw Salve

You will need 6 Tablespoons of Devil's Claw Infused Oil (See RESOURCES for directions on how to make your own Infused Oil)

1 Tablespoon of beeswax

1 Teaspoon of Cocoa Butter

In a pan, add the ingredients and place over low heat, slowly mixing as the beeswax melts.

Once the beeswax is melted and the other ingredients are thoroughly mixed pour the mixture into a clean glass jar with a lid. Store in a cool dark place.

Apply to the areas of pain as needed.

Be sure to check with your medical doctor before using Devil's Claw. See RESOURCES for a list of drugs with which Devil's Claw negatively interacts.

BOSWELLIA

This tree is the source of the Biblical "Frankincense" and is now viewed as a significant treatment for chronic pain.

Making Frankincense Tea

Add 1 tablespoon of Frankincense resin to a one-quart glass jar

Fill the jar with distilled water. Be sure to fill to the very top of the jar.

Add the lid and make sure it is on tight. Keep out of the sunlight.

Let this sit for at least 8 hours. Preferably overnight.

Drink 1 ounce three times a day.

DO NOT THROW OUT THE Frankincense Resin. Add more distilled water and follow the procedures listed above. You can do this 3 times before there is a need to replace the Frankincense Resin.

Making Frankincense Salve

For those who prefer a direct application, creating a Frankincense Salve may be the solution. You will need the following:

- Frankincense Resin Powdered (1 TBS)
- Beeswax (2oz)
- Cocoa Butter (1 oz)
- Rose, Lavender, or Cedar Essential Oil (1 to 2 drops)
- Pot
- Clean, sterilized small jars with lids (2 oz size)

<u>Directions</u>

Add the beeswax and Cocoa Butter to the pot. Place on low heat

Add the Frankincense Resin

Add the essential oil

Stir until all ingredients are thoroughly mixed

Carefully pour the mixture into the jar, let it cool, and add the lid.

Wait a couple of hours before applying it to the area of pain. Apply as needed

Note: This is a small batch. You can make larger quantities. Experiment.

GINGER

Because Ginger has anti-inflammatory properties it may help reduce pain. If you are considering using Ginger for your health you should consult your medical doctor first. Ginger may create negative interactions with any other medications you may be taking. Ginger powder is available but my preference is to use fresh Ginger Root.

Ginger Tea (Drink up to 4 cups daily)

You will need a teapot for boiling water (Microwave water in a safe cup)

2 cups of water

Fresh Ginger Root (About a 2-inch slice)

A strainer

1 fresh lemon

1 Tablespoon of raw honey

1 cup and 1 spoon

Directions

Boil the water,

Shred the Ginger Root and place 1 to 2 tablespoons in the strainer

Add 1 tablespoon of lemon juice to your cup

Add 1 tablespoon of honey to your cup

Place the strainer over the cup and add the water.

Steep for 5 to 8 minutes

Remove the strainer, and stir the contents in the cup

Enjoy

Ginger Salve

You will need the following:

• Carrier Oil (Sweet Almond Oil, Macadamia Oil, Olive Oil, Jojoba Oil

• 2 oz beeswax

- 1 teaspoon of shredded Ginger Root (Press it into the spoon to get a full spoonful. You may add more. Your choice.
- Small glass jar with a lid
- Small pan or double boiler
- A strainer

Directions

In a pan, add 2 tablespoons of carrier oil and 1 teaspoon of shredded Fresh Ginger Root. Place the pan on medium heat. Once the temperature is up, lower the heat and cook for a good 5 minutes. Remove from heat, and strain into a small clean dish. Discard the ginger.

Return the pan to medium heat, and add the 1 oz of beeswax. Once it is melted, add the Ginger Carrier Oil. Mix. (You may add two to four drops of Rose or Lavender Essential oil)

Pour the mixture into the glass jar and let it cool. It will solidify.

Apply a small amount to the area of your back that is in pain. Do this anytime you are not comfortable.

The purpose of these herbal treatments is to not cure the cause of the pain in your back BUT to provide relief. a moment of comfort.

ALSO, BY NORMAN W WILSON PhD

Butterflies and All That Jazz with Drs. James G. Massey and James A. Powell

Windows and Images: An Introduction to the Humanities with Drs. James G. Massey and James A. Powell

The Humanities: Contemporary Images

Shamanism: What It's All About

So, You Think You Want to be a Buddhist?

Promethean Necessity and Its Implications for Humanity

DUH! The American Educational Disaster

The Sayings of Esaugetuh: The Master of Breath

A Shaman's Journey Revealed Through Poetry with Gavriel Navarro

The Shaman's Quest

The Shaman's Transformation

The Shaman's War

The Shaman's Genesis

The Shaman's Revelations

The Making of a Shaman

Activating Your Spirit Guide

Healing-The Shaman's Way

How to Make Moral and Ethical Decisions: A Guide

Teas Soups and Salads

Reiki: The Instructor's Manual

Shamanic Healing Book One

Healing-The Shaman's Way Using Crystals Book Two

COURSES AVAILABLE

Dr. Wilson currently has 3 courses available at Udemy.Com. The first course, Healing-The Shaman's Way is a 17-video lecture program detailing healing techniques such as the use of sound, crystals, essential oils, and herbs.

The second course, Healing-The Shaman's Way Using Crystals details the use of crystals in healing, baking, drinks, and cosmetics. It is a 10-video lecture course loaded with recipes for making elixirs, etc.

The third course, Healing-The Shaman's Way Using Herbs is an 8-video lecture program detailing the use of herbs for the control of pain.